W9-DEZ-015

Golden Eagles

By JoAnn Early Macken

Reading Consultant: Jeanne Clidas, Ph.D.
Director, Roberts Wesleyan College Literacy Clinic

WEEKLY READER®
PUBLISHING

Please visit our web site at **www.garethstevens.com.**
For a free catalog describing our list of high-quality books,
call 1-877-542-2595 (USA) or 1-800-387-3178 (Canada).
Our fax: 1-877-542-2596

Library of Congress Cataloging-in-Publication Data

Macken, JoAnn Early, 1953–
      Golden eagles / by JoAnn Early Macken. — [Rev. ed.]
            p. cm. — (Animals that live in the mountains)
      Includes bibliographical references and index.
      ISBN-10: 1-4339-2413-7   ISBN-13: 978-1-4339-2413-2 (lib. bdg.)
      ISBN-10: 1-4339-2496-X   ISBN-13: 978-1-4339-2496-5 (soft cover)
      1. Golden eagle—Juvenile literature. I. Title.
   QL696.F32M253   2009
   598.9'42—dc22   2009000104

This edition first published in 2010 by
Weekly Reader® Books
An Imprint of Gareth Stevens Publishing
1 Reader's Digest Road
Pleasantville, NY 10570-7000 USA

Executive Managing Editor: Lisa M. Herrington
Senior Editor: Barbara Bakowski
Project Management: Spooky Cheetah Press
Cover Designers: Jennifer Ryder-Talbot and Studio Montage
Production: Studio Montage
Library Consultant: Carl Harvey, Library Media Specialist, Noblesville, Indiana

Photo credits: Cover, pp. 1, 9, 11, 19 Shutterstock; pp. 5, 13, 17 © Tom and Pat Leeson;
p. 7 © Yuri Shibnev/naturepl.com; p. 15 Digital Stock; p. 21 © Alan and Sandy Carey

Printed in the United States of America

1 2 3 4 5 6 7 8 9 14 13 12 11 10 09

Table of Contents

Boldface words appear in the glossary.

Baby Eagles

Golden eagles build huge nests. Each year, they add more sticks. Baby eagles are called **eaglets**. They hatch in the nests.

eaglet

An eaglet has soft feathers called **down**. Its father brings it meat to eat. Its mother feeds it small pieces.

down

Feathers and Flying

Eagles start to fly in about three months. They fly and hunt during the day. At night, they rest in trees.

Golden eagles have gold feathers on their heads and necks. Feathers cover their legs.

legs

A golden eagle can hear well. It listens for other eagles. It listens for storms. If an eagle gets wet, it may not be able to fly.

Strong Hunters

A golden eagle may fly
many miles to find food.
It can spot **prey** from
far away.

Eagles dive from the sky. They catch their prey with claws called **talons**.

talons

Eagles have strong hooked **beaks**. They tear their prey apart. Golden eagles hunt rabbits and mice. They also eat lizards and birds.

beak

In winter, golden eagles may fly to warmer places to find food. They follow their prey down the mountains. In spring, the eagles fly back up.

Fast Facts

Height	about 3 feet (1 meter)
Wingspan	about 7 feet (2 meters)
Weight	about 15 pounds (7 kilograms)
Diet	birds and other small animals
Average life span	up to 20 years

Glossary

beaks: the bills of birds

down: soft, fluffy feathers

eaglets: baby eagles

prey: animals that are killed for food

talons: claws

For More Information

Books

Eagles. New Naturebooks (series). Patrick Merrick (Child's World, 2006)

Those Excellent Eagles. Jan Lee Wicker (Pineapple Press, 2006)

Web Sites

Golden Eagle

www.birds.cornell.edu/AllAboutBirds/BirdGuide/ Golden_Eagle_dtl.html
Listen to sound files of an eagle's call.

Golden Eagle

www.baldeagleinfo.com/eagle/eagle7.html
Watch a video of a golden eagle.

Index

About the Author

JoAnn Early Macken is the author of two rhyming picture books, *Sing-Along Song* and *Cats on Judy*, and more than 80 nonfiction books for children. Her poems have appeared in several children's magazines. She lives in Wisconsin with her husband and their two sons.